BASKETBALL

Blaine Wiseman

www.av2books.com

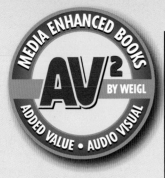

BOOK CODE

N518858

AV² by Weigl brings you media enhanced books that support active learning.

AV² provides enriched content that supplements and complements this book. Weigl's AV² books strive to create inspired learning and engage young minds for a total learning experience.

Go to **www.av2books.com**, and enter this book's unique code. You will have access to video, audio, web links, quizzes, a slide show, and activities.

Audio
Listen to sections of the book read aloud.

Video
Watch informative video clips.

Web Link
Find research sites and play interactive games.

Try This!
Complete activities and hands-on experiments.

Due to the dynamic nature of the Internet, some of the URLs and activities provided as part of AV² by Weigl may have changed or ceased to exist. AV² by Weigl accepts no responsibility for any such changes. All media enhanced books are regularly monitored to update addresses and sites in a timely manner. Contact AV² by Weigl at 1-866-649-3445 or av2books@weigl.com with any questions, comments, or feedback.

Published by AV² by Weigl
350 5ᵗʰ Avenue, 59ᵗʰ Floor
New York, NY 10118
Website: www.av2books.com   www.weigl.com

Library of Congress Cataloging-in-Publication Data

Wiseman, Blaine.
 Basketball / Blaine Wiseman.
   p. cm. -- (Record breakers)
 Includes index.
 ISBN 978-1-61690-118-9 (hardcover : alk. paper) -- ISBN 978-1-61690-119-6 (softcover : alk. paper) -- ISBN 978-1-61690-120-2 (e-book)
 1. Basketball--Records--Juvenile literature. 2. Basketball players--Juvenile literature. I. Title.
 GV885.1.W56 2011
 796.323--dc22
                    2010006154

Printed in the United States of America in North Mankato, Minnesota
1 2 3 4 5 6 7 8 9 0 14 13 12 11 10

052010
WEP264000

Project Coordinator Heather C. Hudak
Design Terry Paulhus

Photo Credits
Every reasonable effort has been made to trace ownership and to obtain permission to reprint copyright material. The publishers would be pleased to have any errors or omissions brought to their attention so that they may be corrected in subsequent printings.

Contents

The Shooters

Michael Jordan is one of the most exciting, effective basketball players of all-time. He led the Chicago Bulls to six National Basketball Association (NBA) championships and broke many records throughout his career. "Air Jordan" is best known for his dunking ability and his **clutch** shooting. These are some of Jordan's basketball records.

Michael Jordan's Records

Points per game (regular season) – 30.1
Tied with Wilt Chamberlain

Points per game (playoffs) – 33.45
Allen Iverson of the Philadelphia 76ers is second, averaging 29.73 points.

Most points in a playoff game – 63
After the game, Boston Celtics legend Larry Bird said that Jordan was "God disguised as Michael Jordan."

NBA scoring titles – 10
Three more than Chamberlain held

Career points (playoffs) – 5,987
Kareem Abdul-Jabbar is second with 5,762.

NBA Finals Most Valuable Player (MVP) awards – 6
Magic Johnson, Shaquille O'Neal, and Tim Duncan are tied for second, with three each.

Michael Jordan

Woman's Game

The Women's National Basketball Association (WNBA) is a professional basketball league for women. The WNBA began in 1997 and has entertained millions of fans with highly skilled and competitive basketball. While the WNBA is a fairly young league, many scoring records have been set and broken by its athletes.

Seimone Augustus

Basket Cases

In order to score 30,000 points in the NBA, a player must dominate other teams for a long period of time. These players were the greatest of their time.

Player	Points
Kareem Abdul-Jabbar Milwaukee Bucks Los Angeles Lakers	38,387
Karl Malone Utah Jazz Los Angeles Lakers	36,928
Michael Jordan Chicago Bulls Washington Wizards	32,292
Wilt Chamberlain Philadelphia/San Francisco Warriors Philadelphia 76ers Los Angeles Lakers	31,419
Shaquille O'Neal Orlando Magic Los Angeles Lakers Miami Heat Phoenix Suns Cleveland Cavaliers	28, 229

WNBA Records

Points – 6,263
Lisa Leslie, Los Angeles Sparks

Points per game – 21.25
Seimone Augustus, Minnesota Lynx

Games played – 378
Vickie Johnson, New York Liberty,
San Antonio Silver Stars

Three-pointers – 674
Katie Smith, Minnesota Lynx Detroit, Tulsa Shock

Assists – 2,023
Ticha Penicheiro, Sacramento Monarchs

Karl Malone

The Defenders

Big Blocks

A block is an important defensive play in basketball. It stops a basket and can turn the game around for the defensive team. The best blockers are big, strong players with fast reflexes. Here are the NBA all-time career leaders in blocks.

Best Blockers

Hakeem Olajuwon – 3,830
Houston Rockets, Toronto Raptors

Dikembe Mutombo – 3,289
Denver Nuggets, Atlanta Hawks,
Philadelphia 76ers, New Jersey Nets,
New York Knicks, Houston Rockets

Kareem Abdul-Jabbar – 3,189
Milwaukee Bucks, Los Angeles Lakers

Mark Eaton – 3,064
Utah Jazz

David Robinson – 2,954
San Antonio Spurs

Hakeem Olajuwon

Fast Steals

In basketball, stealing is a great play. When players make a steal, their team turns from defense to offense. These players had the most steals in their careers.

John Stockton – 3,265
Utah Jazz

Michael Jordan – 2,514
Chicago Bulls, Washington Wizards

Gary Payton – 2,445
Seattle Supersonics, Milwaukee Bucks,
Los Angeles Lakers, Boston Celtics, Miami Heat

Maurice Cheeks – 2,310
Philadelphia 76ers, San Antonio Spurs, New York
Knicks, Atlanta Hawks, New Jersey Nets

Scottie Pippen – 2,307
Chicago Bulls, Houston Rockets, Portland Trail Blazers

Girl Guards

These WNBA players hold records in the areas of rebounds, blocks, and steals.

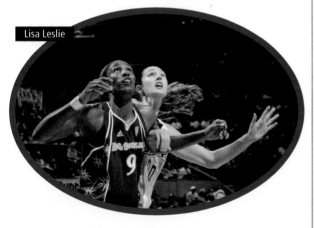
Lisa Leslie

Most rebounds – 3,156
Lisa Leslie, Los Angeles Sparks

Most blocks – 877
Margo Dydek, Utah Starzz, San Antonio Silver
Stars, Connecticut Suns, Los Angeles Sparks

Most steals – 655
Ticha Penicheiro, Sacramento Monarchs

Board Work

When a basketball hits the rim or the backboard, players jump up to grab the ball before the other team can get it. An offensive rebound is when the shooting team gets the ball. A defensive rebound happens when the team playing defense gets the ball first. Here are the best rebounders of all time.

Wilt Chamberlain

Wilt Chamberlain – 23,924 rebounds
Philadelphia/San Francisco Warriors,
Philadelphia 76ers, Los Angeles Lakers

Bill Russell – 21,620
Boston Celtics

Kareem Abdul-Jabbar – 17,440
Milwaukee Bucks, Los Angeles Lakers

Elvin Hayes – 16,279
San Diego/Houston Rockets,
Baltimore/Washington Bullets, Houston Rockets

Moses Malone – 16,212
Buffalo Braves, Houston Rockets, Philadelphia
76ers, Washington Bullets, Atlanta Hawks,
Milwaukee Bucks, San Antonio Spurs

The Coaches

Phil the Thrill

There have been many great coaches throughout NBA history. Phil Jackson, who coaches the Los Angeles Lakers, is the most successful of these legendary leaders. Throughout his career, Jackson has won a record 70.5 percent of his games and holds the record for most championships. In Chicago, Jackson coached Michael Jordan and the Bulls to six NBA championships. Since joining Kobe Bryant and the Lakers, Jackson has won three more titles. During his career, Jackson also has won more playoff games than any other coach.

Knight and Day

Throughout his coaching career in the National Collegiate Athletic Association (NCAA), Bobby Knight was known as a winner. Starting his career coaching Army, Knight moved to Indiana to coach the Hoosiers from 1971 until 2000. He finished his career with Texas Tech, breaking the record for most wins in college basketball. When Knight retired in 2008, he had 902 wins, 371 losses, and three NCAA championships.

Wilkens the Winner

Coaching in the NBA is a difficult job. It takes strong leadership, work ethic, patience, and knowledge to be a great coach. Lenny Wilkens played in the league from 1960 until 1975. He began coaching while playing with Seattle and later with Portland. Wilkens also coached in Cleveland, Atlanta, Toronto, and New York. He won more career games than any other coach. In 1989, Wilkens was **inducted** into the Hall of Fame as a player. He made the Hall of Fame as a coach in 1998.

The Championship

Sizing It Up

Each spring, the NBA playoffs end when one team is crowned champion and presented with the Larry O'Brien NBA Championship trophy. Winning the famed golden trophy is the goal of every basketball player. Each year, the trophy is made in New York City by Tiffany & Co., the same company that makes the Super Bowl and World Series championship trophies. The trophy, which is made of sterling silver and covered in gold, weighs about 16 pounds (7.3 kilograms) and stands 2 feet (0.6 meters) tall. The trophy is made to look like a life-size basketball on the rim of a basket.

Michael Jordan

TROPHY COLLECTORS ★

It takes a skilled team with talented players to win multiple NBA championships. The Boston Celtics' Bill Russell won 11 championships in his 13-year career to lead the list of players with the most championship titles.

Bill Russell

Since their first title in 1957, the Boston Celtics have won championships in every decade, except the 1990s. The Celtics have won more titles than any other team. They dominated the game for more than a decade in the 1950s and 1960s. The Celtics record 17th league championship came in 2008, when they defeated the Los Angeles Lakers. With 15 wins, the Lakers are second on the list of teams with the most championship titles.

Player	Championships	Team
Bill Russell	11	Boston Celtics
Sam Jones	10	Boston Celtics
John Havlicek	8	Boston Celtics
Tom Heinsohn	8	Boston Celtics
KC Jones	8	Boston Celtics
Tom Sanders	8	Boston Celtics

Streaks

The Celtics have won more consecutive league titles than any other team, with eight in a row from 1959 until 1966.

Boston Celtics – 17
1957, 1959–1966, 1968, 1969, 1974, 1976,1981, 1984, 1986, 2008

Los Angeles Lakers – 15
1949, 1950, 1952–1954, 1972, 1980, 1982,1985, 1987, 1988, 2000–2002, 2009

Chicago Bulls – 6
1991–1993, 1996–1998

San Antonio Spurs – 4
1999, 2003, 2005, 2007

Detroit Pistons – 3
1989, 1990, 2004

The second-longest streak is three years in a row. This has been done a total of four times by only two teams. The Bulls won three straight titles from 1991 until 1993, and then again from 1996 to 1998. The Lakers' first streak came in the 1950s. They did it again from 2000 to 2002, led by Kobe Bryant and Shaquille O'Neal.

Magic Johnson

The Gear

NBA uniforms feature sleeveless shirts and long, baggy shorts that are designed to help players keep cool. Every uniform features the team's logo and colors, as well as the name and number of the player. The uniforms worn today are different than uniforms worn in the past. The first basketball players wore long, baggy pants. Early jerseys were long and could be buttoned between the legs, to keep them tucked into the pants.

Wilt Chamberlain

In the 1970s and 1980s, uniforms were very tight. The shorts only came about halfway down the players' thighs. When Michael Jordan began wearing looser, longer shorts, other players did the same.

Peach Basketball

The game of basketball was invented in 1891 by Dr. James Naismith, a teacher in Springfield, Massachusetts. The first game was played using peach baskets, giving it the name basketball. With each point that was scored, the janitor would climb a ladder to retrieve the ball from the basket. Soon, a metal rim with a net hanging from the bottom replaced the peach baskets. However, the net was closed at the bottom. In 1906, the net was cut open. The open net is still used today.

Bouncy Balls

Naismith invented basketball using other sports for inspiration. At first, players used a soccer ball. Soon, people began making special balls by stitching leather around a rubber **bladder**. Molded basketballs were first made in the 1940s. These balls are made in a factory from a mold, which makes each ball exactly the same. This allowed players to become more skilled at the sport because every ball bounced the same.

Sneaky Guys

Basketball sneakers are another piece of equipment that combine style with function. Originally, basketball players wore low-cut, canvas shoes. Starting in the 1920s, Chuck Taylors became the most popular basketball shoe. These shoes were made of **canvas** with rubber **soles**. In 1984, a shoe named after Michael Jordan made basketball sneakers a major industry. The "Air Jordan" made by Nike became the most popular sneaker **brand**. Today, many NBA stars, such as Kobe Bryant and LeBron James, have their own brand of sneakers.

13

More Records

Manute Bol

Spud Webb

Skyscrapers

Most often, basketball players are tall. Their height puts them closer to the net. The average height in the NBA is about 6 feet 7 inches (1.9 meters). These players are the tallest to ever play in the NBA.

Margo Dydek, who plays for the Los Angeles Sparks, is one of the tallest women in the world. At 7 feet 2 inches (5 centimeters), she is one inch (2.5 cm) taller than Shaquille O'Neal and is the tallest woman in the WNBA.

Manute Bol – 7 feet 7 inches (2.3 m)
Washington Bullets, Golden State Warriors, Philadelphia 76ers, Miami Heat

Gheorghe Muresan – 7 feet 7 inches (2.3 m)
Washington Bullets, New Jersey Nets

Shawn Bradley – 7 feet 6 inches (2.28 m)
Philadelphia 76ers, New Jersey
Nets, Dallas Mavericks

Yao Ming – 7 feet 6 inches (2.28 m)
Houston Rockets

Chuck Nevitt – 7 feet 5 inches (2.26 m)
Houston Rockets, Los Angeles Lakers, Detroit Pistons, Chicago Bulls, San Antonio Spurs

Yao Ming

Earl Boykins

Big Impact

Even though being tall is a definite advantage in basketball, many shorter players have made a big impact on the game. These men made a big difference in the NBA.

Muggsy Bogues – 5 feet 3 inches
Washington Bullets, Charlotte Hornets, Golden State Warriors, Toronto Raptors. The shortest player ever in the NBA. He had a 14-season career and could dunk the ball into the 10-foot (3 m) high net.

Earl Boykins – 5 feet 5 inches
New Jersey Nets, Cleveland Cavaliers, Orlando Magic, Los Angeles Clippers, Golden State Warriors, Denver Nuggets, Milwaukee Bucks, Charlotte Bobcats, Washington Wizards. Won the NBA Slam Dunk Contest.

Spud Webb – 5 feet 7 inches
Atlanta Hawks, Sacramento Kings, Minnesota Timberwolves, Orlando Magic. Holds the record for most points in one overtime, with 15.

College Life

Millions of fans watch the future stars of the NBA play for their college teams. Most great basketball players have attended college. Here are some NCAA Division I records.

Most career points – 3,667
"Pistol" Pete Maravich, Louisiana State

Most career rebounds – 1,570
Tim Duncan, Wake Forest

Most career assists – 1,076
Bobby Hurley, Duke

Most career blocks – 535
Wojciech Mydra, Louisiana-Monroe

Most career steals – 385
John Linehan, Providence

Mr. Assist

Players who score highlight reel baskets usually get more attention than the players who set them up for the basket. **Playmakers** like to stay hidden, making great plays by finding open teammates. These players are the NBA's leaders in all-time career assists.

John Stockton

John Stockton – 15,806
Utah Jazz

Jason Kidd – 10,712
Dallas Mavericks, Phoenix Suns, New Jersey Nets

Mark Jackson – 10,334
New York Knicks, Los Angeles Clippers, Indiana Pacers, Denver Nuggets, Toronto Raptors, Utah Jazz, Houston Rockets

Magic Johnson – 10,141
Los Angeles Lakers

Oscar Robertson – 9,887
Cincinnati Royals, Milwaukee Bucks

Tim Duncan

15

Most Valuable Players

In the NBA, the top honor for individual performance is to be named Most Valuable Player (MVP). At the end of each regular season, the MVP is awarded to the player who has been most important to his team's success.

Here is a list of the players who have won the award more times than any other players in NBA history.

Larry Bird

MVP 3 Times

Born: Bedford, Indiana
Position: Forward
MVP: 1984, 1985, 1986
Team: Boston Celtics

Bill Russell

MVP 5 Times

Born: Monroe, Louisiana
Position: Center
MVP: 1958, 1961, 1962, 1963, 1965
Team: Boston Celtics

Pacific Ocean

N
W E
S

140 Miles
0   225 Kilometers

Wilt Chamberlain

MVP 4 Times

Born:
Philadelphia, Pennsylvania
Position: Center
MVP: 1960
Team: Philadelphia Warriors
MVP: 1966, 1967, 1968
Team: Philadelphia 76ers

Michael Jordan

MVP 5 Times

Born:
Brooklyn, New York
Position: Shooting Guard
MVP: 1988, 1991, 1992,1996,1998,
Team: Chicago Bulls

Moses Malone

MVP 3 Times

Born:
Petersburg, Virginia
Position: Center/Power Forward
MVP: 1979, 1982
Team: Houston Rockets
MVP: 1983
Team: Philadelphia 76ers

Kareem Abdul-Jabbar

MVP 6 Times

Born:
Harlem, New York
Position: Center
MVP: 1971, 1972, 1974
Team: Milwaukee Bucks
MVP: 1976, 1977, 1980
Team: Los Angeles Lakers

Atlantic
Ocean

UNITED
STATES

The Hardwood

Al Harrington

The Garden

Basketball is a game with many traditions. Most NBA teams play in newer stadiums. The New York Knicks, however, have always played in the same stadium. Since they helped form the Basketball Association of America in 1946, the Knicks have played at Madison Square Garden (MSG). In 1968, MSG was rebuilt, and the Knicks have called the new version of the building home ever since. Nearby, the New Jersey Nets played in the same building from 1981 to 2010. The Izod Center is the league's second oldest stadium.

Brooklyn Bound

At the beginning of the 2010 to 2011 season, the Nets moved to a new stadium in Brooklyn, New York. The Barclays Center was designed by well-known architect, Frank Gehry. The Nets are the first professional sports team to call Brooklyn home since baseball's Brooklyn Dodgers moved to Los Angeles in 1957.

New Building on the Block

The newest stadium in the NBA belongs to the newest team. In 2005, the Charlotte Bobcats opened their first season at the brand new Time Warner Cable Arena. Known as the "TWC Arena," the arena was built to host Charlotte's second NBA team, after the Hornets moved to New Orleans in 2002. The $260 million building can hold 19,026 fans for NBA games and 20,200 for college basketball games.

The Biggest Barns

Stadium	Team	Seats
The Palace of Auburn Hills	Detroit Pistons	22,076
Wachovia Center	Philadelphia 76ers	21,600
United Center	Chicago Bulls	21,500
American Airlines Center	Dallas Mavericks	21,041
Rose Garden	Portland Trail Blazers	20,630

In The Money

Basketball players are highly paid. These are the highest paid athletes in the sport.

Tracy McGrady
Houston Rockets - $23.3 million

Kobe Bryant
Los Angeles Lakers - $23 million

Jermaine O'Neal
Miami Heat - $22.9 million

Tim Duncan
San Antonio Spurs - $22.2 million

Shaquille O'Neal
Cleveland Cavaliers - $20 million

BIG BUSINESS

NBA teams are businesses. People pay large amounts of money to own basketball teams. These are the most valuable NBA teams.

New York Knicks – $613 million

Los Angeles Lakers – $584 million

Chicago Bulls – $504 million

Detroit Pistons – $480 million

Cleveland Cavaliers – $477 million

Tracy McGrady

Spending at the Game

On average, how much do people spend at a basketball game?
Ticket: $50
Hot dog: $4
Soft drink: $3.50
Program: $3.50
Hat: $15

Culture

In the NBA, the best seats in the house are right on the floor, front row, at court level. These seats, called courtside seats, are difficult to get and can cost large amounts of money. It is common to see celebrities cheering on their favorite teams from courtside seats. Hollywood actor Jack Nicholson is often found cheering from the front row at Lakers games. Film directors Spike Lee and Woody Allen are two of the best-known courtside faces at Knicks games. These fans pay thousands of dollars each game to sit in these seats.

Pickup Basketball

Basketball is a great game to enjoy outdoors. Many parks in cities around the world have become venues for games of three-on-three, five-on-five, 21, horse, and many other types of basketball games. The NBA hosted an outdoor game in San Juan, Puerto Rico, between Milwaukee and Phoenix in 1972. The next outdoor NBA game was in 2008, when the Suns played the Denver Nuggets in a **preseason** game at the Indian Wells Tennis Garden in Indian Wells, California.

Mascot Madness

Mascots are an entertaining part of basketball games. Crazy characters run around the arena exciting the fans and performing stunts. Sometimes, mascots become part of the game. In 2009, during a playoff game between the Atlanta Hawks and the Miami Heat, Atlanta's mascot, a real hawk, named "Spirit," was released to fly around the stadium. Spirit would not stop flying around, and the game had to be delayed.

21

QUIZ

1 Who has won the most NBA Finals MVP awards?

2 Who holds the WNBA record for steals?

3 What NCAA coach holds the record for wins?

4 What Boston Celtic won more NBA championships than any other player?

5 What year did James Naismith invent basketball?

6 What was the last professional sports team in Brooklyn before the Nets?

7 Who has been given the most MVP awards?

8 Who is the shortest player in NBA history?

9 What NBA team is the most valuable?

10 Where did the first outdoor NBA game take place?

ANSWERS: 1. Michael Jordan 2. Lisa Leslie 3. Bobby Knight 4. Bill Russell 5. 1891 6. The Dodgers 7. Kareem Abdul-Jabbar 8. Muggsy Bogues 9. New York Knicks 10. San Juan, Puerto Rico

GLOSSARY

bladder: an object that holds liquid or air

brand: a product with a particular name, made by a certain company

canvas: a strong type of cloth

clutch: being reliable at an important event

inducted: chosen or included to be admitted into a position or an organization

MVP: most valuable player

playmakers: players who create scoring chances for teammates

preseason: games used as tryouts or warmups before the regular season

soles: the bottoms of shoes

INDEX

Log on to www.av2books.com

AV² by Weigl brings you media enhanced books that support active learning. Go to **www.av2books.com**, and enter the special code inside the front cover of this book. You will gain access to enriched and enhanced content that supplements and complements this book. Content includes video, audio, web links, quizzes, a slide show, and activities.

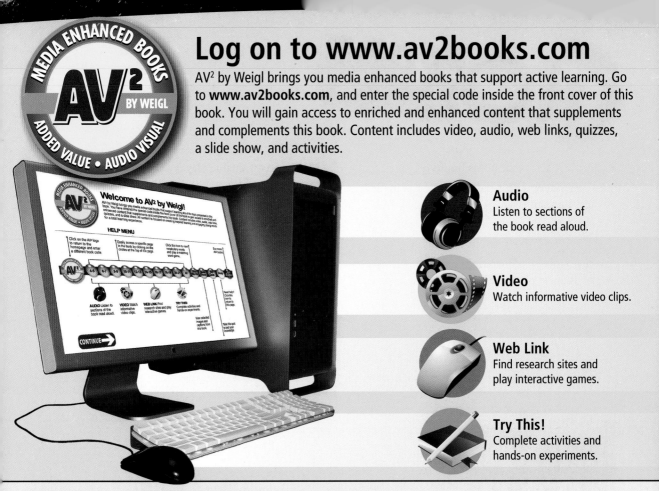

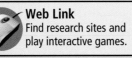

Audio
Listen to sections of the book read aloud.

Video
Watch informative video clips.

Web Link
Find research sites and play interactive games.

Try This!
Complete activities and hands-on experiments.

WHAT'S ONLINE?

Try This! Complete activities and hands-on experiments.	Web Link Find research sites and play interactive games.	Video Watch informative video clips.	EXTRA FEATURES
Pages 10-11 Try this basketball activity.	**Pages 6-7** Learn more about basketball players.	**Pages 4-5** Watch a video about basketball.	**Audio** Hear introductory audio at the top of every page
Pages 12-13 Test your knowledge of basketball gear.	**Pages 8-9** Read about basketball coaches.	**Pages 14-15** View stars of the sport in action.	**Key Words** Study vocabulary, and play a matching word game.
Pages 16-17 Complete this mapping activity.	**Pages 18-19** Find out more about where basketball games take place.	**Pages 20-21** Watch a video about basketball players.	**Slide Show** View images and captions, and try a writing activity.
			AV² Quiz Take this quiz to test your knowledge